Behind the Microscope
Solving Scientific Mysteries

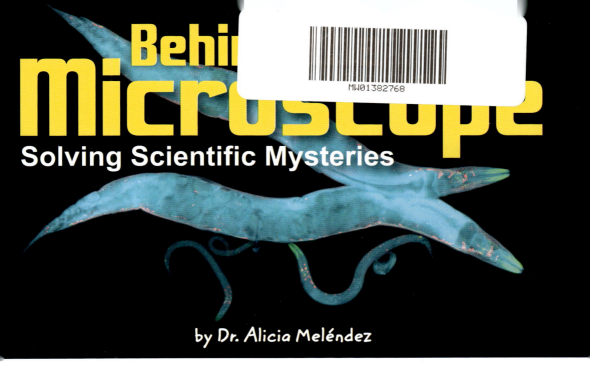

by Dr. Alicia Meléndez

Table of Contents

2 Introduction

4 Educating a Scientist

17 At Work Today

27 Succeeding in Science and Beyond

31 Glossary

32 Analyze the Text

Introduction

Welcome to my lab at Queens College in New York City! As you can see, it's named for me, Dr. Alicia Meléndez. I'm a professor in the **biology** department. Here in the lab, my students and I work with worms—not earthworms, but roundworms, whose formal name is *Caenorhabditis elegans* (*C. elegans* for short). That's a mouthful! So my students and I just call them "worms."

We observe these worms to learn how their cells grow and communicate because these worms' cells are like human cells in some ways. Studying worms can help us understand humans; for example, have you ever wondered why people get old—why our bodies slow down and change? I would like to know how this happens. This is the basis of my research with worms.

As a little girl, people asked me if I wanted to be a doctor or a lawyer or a police officer when I grew up. I knew I wanted to do research—to investigate and find new facts—but I didn't know that there was a word for that. I didn't know that meant I wanted to be a scientist. I even remember asking my father when I was five years old, "What do you call that?" because I knew there must be a name for that job!

I'm kind of a nerd because I always loved science and I always wanted to do research. I just liked the idea of learning something that nobody else knew; I thought that was the coolest thing. I still do.

me in my lab

Why Worms?

C. elegans are used by scientists because they are easy to care for and study; you can see right through them. Worms are simple organisms, so we can isolate what we want to look at. Worms are also easy to house; thousands can fit on a single Petri dish. They are cheap to keep, too, as they feed on bacteria.

Educating a Scientist

I grew up in San Juan, Puerto Rico, and went to Cupeyville School, in the Cupey *barrio*, or neighborhood, of that city. It was an English-speaking school, but we spoke Spanish at home. As a child, I was very competitive in school. I always competed against the two or three boys who seemed to know more than I did; I was really motivated to do better than them.

I remember an activity in fifth grade where one of my favorite teachers, Ms. Santini, had us write a review or summary of every book we read, and I worked so hard to have as many entries as possible. Ms. Santini became a great **mentor** to me after that, and we were very close for years.

San Juan, Puerto Rico, my original hometown

My real interest as a kid was scientific research, although I didn't know what that was at the time. I thought doing science research was like being a doctor. Fortunately, I had people in my family who encouraged my curiosity and interests; my grandfather was one of my most ardent supporters—and best guinea pigs. He had no serious **ailments**, thank goodness, but I would "cure" him of pretend aches and pains by putting a mentholated cream and a bright red antiseptic solution on his toes. Then I would bandage each toe, and he would walk around hobbling and nodding and smiling, as if he felt better already. He even had a special name for me in Spanish: he would greet me at the door saying, *La doctora casilda!* (the house doctor).

My kindergarten graduation! I am wearing a special dress for dancing to *Plena*, a type of folk music in Puerto Rico.

I loved many things that other kids were into at that age as well, such as watching TV. I especially liked the shows featuring Jacques Cousteau, the famous scientist and explorer of oceans, and his undersea adventures. Discovering and learning to understand a new world seemed so cool to me. I must admit, however, I also watched Puerto Rican soap operas with my grandmother. There was one called *Cristina Bazan,* which was among the first to be produced in Puerto Rico.

As a kid, I loved watching *The Undersea World of Jacques Cousteau* TV shows.

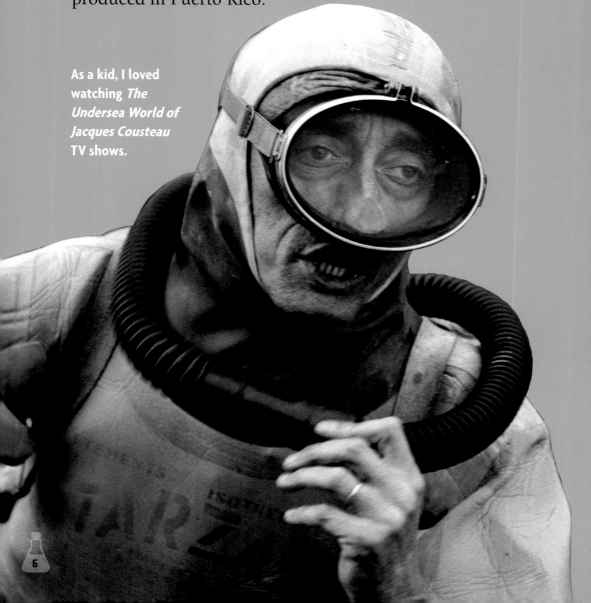

In addition to my studies, I participated in after school clubs and tutored a girl who was younger than me. I got my first real introduction to biology in fifth grade. That subject really intrigued me because I was already so fascinated with how nature and our bodies work.

Because I was a good student at Cupeyville School, and because in my school it was sort of expected that good students would go abroad to the United States for college, I remember around sixth grade or so my father saying, "You are going to go abroad. There is no question in my mind that you are going to go." My mother also encouraged me to aspire to a college in the United States, even though I was her firstborn child and only girl.

Here I am at my high school graduation. My teacher and mentor, Ms. Santini, is presenting me with an academic award.

My parents were right about me. In 1983, I left for Princeton University in Princeton, New Jersey. I felt pretty smart when I got there because I was only the second student from Cupeyville School to be accepted by this highly selective Ivy League college. Yet even though I had been a strong student and loved science, I learned quickly that university classes were not easy. My science classes were so hard for me when I first arrived that I actually considered picking a different course of study. Politics and philosophy appealed to me because I liked to read about political ideas, and about women in politics and the position of women in society. I even took all the required courses for a **major** in political philosophy, but in the end came back to science. I thought, *Well, I can always read about politics, but I cannot do experiments in my backyard!*

I attended Princeton University in New Jersey from 1983 to 1987.

So that's how I chose to study science, and soon my career began to take shape. At Princeton I had the good fortune to study under Eric Wieschaus, who later won the prestigious Nobel Prize. His work involved studying the early development of fruit flies. He studied how **mutants** would not follow the normal process of development. It sounds funny to talk about mutants, but there was nothing more interesting to me in the world than that! It was in Dr. Wieschaus's class that I got hooked on research.

Then came time to write my **thesis**. I had the choice to write a library thesis or a research thesis. A library thesis requires that you go to the library and get all the information that has already been published on a specific subject and then write about other people's work. For a research thesis, you come up with a hypothesis, then go into the lab to do the experiments yourself. Naturally, I chose a research thesis.

In 1995, my mentor, Dr. Eric F. Wieschaus, shared a Nobel Prize in Physiology and Medicine with his fellow researchers Christiane Nüsslein-Volhard and Edward B. Lewis for their discoveries concerning the genetic control of embryonic development.

My college pals and I are at the Princeton University graduation "P-rade." I am on the left, wearing our school colors. Go Tigers!

My research thesis at Princeton was not about bandaging my grandfather's toes and getting a smile—not at all. I developed my own studies, carried out the research, and reported the results. The wonderful thing was that I was taken seriously; I was asserting my scientific point of view. I recall how excited I was when Christiane Nüsslein-Volhard, a **prominent** female scientist, came to visit the lab. I had an appointment with her and showed her my data. It was an amazing experience as an undergraduate to discuss my research with an established person in the field.

That's also when I began to understand the importance of genetics, a scientific field related to biology that focuses on heredity. Genetics shows us why some animals can't grow or function properly. By doing that, genetics also helps us understand how animals *do* grow and function properly.

I also discovered that the upper level of scientific research became more competitive; more and more, I was surrounded by men. As much as I loved my studies, being a woman scientist wasn't easy—especially a woman Puerto Rican scientist. It was when I was in college that I realized for the first time I wasn't in the mainstream, I was a **minority**. Yet I didn't quite understand fully what that meant. It was unnerving and a bit shocking at first because I had grown up in the majority all my life, being Hispanic in Puerto Rico.

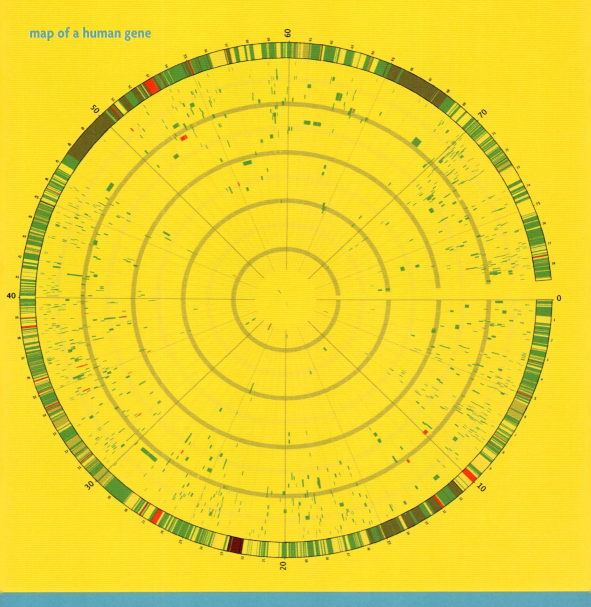

map of a human gene

What is the difference between biology and genetics?

Biology is the study of living organisms: how they eat, how they die, etc., and includes animals and plants. Biology also includes the study of how evolution has shaped animals and plants. Genetics is part of that, but more specific. Genetics is the study of how the basic building blocks of life function; you map them out, and then you figure out how they make organisms what they are.

I encountered this imbalance again after I finished college and went on to seek a PhD in biology. A PhD, or doctorate, is the highest degree a person can earn in school. Although there were more and more females entering science PhD programs than ever at that time, it was totally the opposite regarding the professors at the top of the field: many, many more men had science PhDs than women did. Being a research scientist is so demanding that there is not much time to spend with a family. Many women have felt that they had to choose whether to become a scientist or a mother. Fortunately, some schools are now trying to change this.

But when I was in graduate school, people just did not expect to see women in science at the higher levels for these reasons. Even today, when I go to meetings with my husband, people sometimes assume he is the scientist when we *both* are! There have been times when my husband has been at a meeting with me and someone has approached him as if he is the biologist, and I am not, and he starts laughing. He says "No, I am the sidekick at this meeting!"

me with my husband, Dr. Hannes Bülow

students in a science lab

I earned my PhD and did two fellowships at Columbia University in New York City.

After a scientist gets a PhD, at least in biology, he or she will often do what's called a post-doctoral **fellowship**. It's like a job where you are paid to do an advanced research project. You establish yourself as an independent scientist with your own line of research, but you are still working under someone's direction in their lab. I did two fellowships, both at the medical school at Columbia University in New York City.

During my PhD studies I had used fruit flies for my research. During my first fellowship I switched to using worms for my research so that I could learn about another organism's systems. It is good for biologists to see how different organisms function, plus this was really fun for me.

Yet I still had to deal with other people's stereotypes. One time, during my first fellowship, I worked in a lab where the technician, a fellow Puerto Rican, was always very friendly. After a month into my time there, while helping me move something, he suddenly realized I wasn't just a secretary for someone "important." I was the important one! We laughed about it, but unfortunately this kind of thing happened often, because many people thought that if you were Hispanic you were either a secretary or a janitor.

fruit flies

A Prank

One time, I was working as a technician at a university lab in Cleveland, and my neighboring lab was a fruit fly lab. A researcher there, Peter, came from the neighboring lab with a vial. He had been screening, or looking for, a particular mutant fly. After three months he had found his first, so he came over very excited. He set the vial down and went away for a moment; while he was gone, a friend and I took an empty vial and broke it. When Peter came back we told him, "Your vial fell and broke!" For two hours Peter looked all over the lab, determined to find his little mutant fly again. Finally, we had mercy on him and told him it was a trick! He didn't speak to us for two months. (Now, in retrospect, I can't say I blame him.)

Here I am with my PhD students: Nicholas J. Palmisano, Kristina Ames, and Melissa Silvestrini. At top right, they are at work in the lab.

At Work Today

Today I live in New York City and work at Queens College, a branch of the City University of New York (CUNY), as an associate professor of biology. Actually, my job is more like a few jobs at once! One part of my job is training students to be independent thinkers and researchers in my laboratory. I try to encourage the students in their thesis research projects and guide them through their discovery process. A student may make an observation that sends all of us in a new direction, which is great because sometimes I end up learning, too! Researchers go where the research takes them and sometimes that research comes from students.

Another part of my work is to teach. I teach basic research methods and the genetic approach to research. We try to understand the very basics of how things happen, and how biology works. I usually teach one or one-and-a-half courses a **semester**, so I am in the classroom usually twice a week for two hours or so each time. Teaching at a college level isn't as time-consuming as it is at an elementary, middle, or high school. But teaching is often just as satisfying for me as doing research, especially when I can get a student inspired by the subject.

Providing this type of inspiration and opportunity is very important to me, and part of why I choose to teach at Queens College. As a CUNY school it is a public institution, which means a lot of the funding comes from the government. That makes it much less expensive for students from the local community to attend. I had the option to teach at a private university with more affluent students, but declined. The tuition at Queens is just a few thousand dollars each year; the students are mainly from less wealthy backgrounds and are often **emigrants** themselves or children of emigrants. They offer different perspectives and are highly motivated, which makes my work more enjoyable.

Another big part of my job is to acquire funds to pay for my research. Maintaining a lab and doing experiments is expensive. To conduct experiments, research scientists must obtain grants—funding from the government and other organizations. Writing grant applications is something I am constantly doing. It's a very hard part of my job, and getting harder and more competitive. So far, I have been successful at getting funding and my lab has been continuously funded for the past six years.

Getting the Scoop

Alicia says: "The fun thing about science is the discovery; you could discover something and be the only person in the world who knows it! At least, you hope you are the only one because otherwise, you are going to get scooped."

I am also very involved in running the PhD program at Queens College. Our program works with other schools in the CUNY system to produce graduates who are ready to practice science as professionals.

My student Melissa is extracting genetic information from dying bacteria cells.

A *C. elegans* worm is only one millimeter (three sixty-fourths of an inch), so we need to use a powerful microscope to study them.

My favorite part of work, though, is doing research. After all, I am a research scientist whose favorite tool is a microscope! Much of what I am studying now is how animals age and why. We use worms to study the aging process because worms have a short life span. They typically live up to twenty days, yet acquire many characteristics similar to humans when they age. For example, they get fat, wrinkled, and slow-moving. My focus is on mutations (changes) that allow these worms to live longer. In 2003, I showed that for worms to live longer than usual, they required a process called autophagy. Autophagy (from Greek words meaning "self" and "to eat") is where cells actually recycle part of themselves. In the recycling process, they get rid of material that contributes to their aging, which lets them live longer.

Making discoveries is a fantastic feeling; it is also deeply gratifying to see how my research inspires other scientists, who then take it to another level. In my lab, we have established

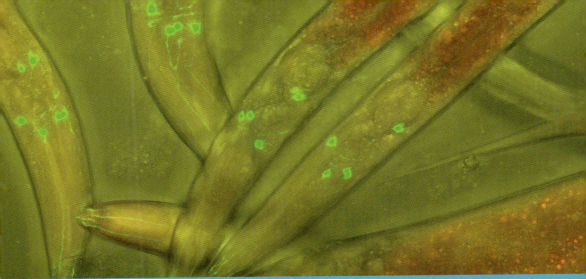

C. elegans is transparent, or easy to see through, which is helpful for our studies. We use a special green fluorescent protein we call "GFP" to help us see the insides of the worm and its body.

some basic workings of autophagy. Now, others are applying what we've learned to studying autophagy in the longevity of mice. They have shown the same thing we learned about worms—that mice whose cells go through autophagy live much longer than expected.

For instance, Dr. Nils Barzilan at Albert Einstein College of Medicine is studying people ninety-five and older to find out what they have in common that allows them to live that long. And guess what? He has some indication that the same healthy aging factors that allow worms to live longer also work in humans. Another scientist at Einstein, Dr. Ana Maria Cuervo, has shown that an increase in autophagy in older mice can be rejuvenating. Yes, science may have found a part of the fountain of youth!

My research on autophagy in worms is being used to study aging in humans.

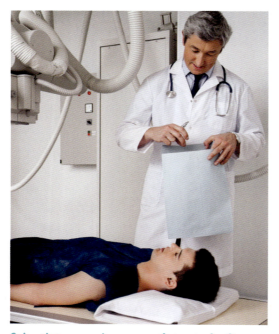

Scientists are using research to study the link between autophagy and cancer.

But our work on aging is only beginning. Some recent studies have shown that caloric restriction, or eating less, helps animals live longer by turning on this process of autophagy—recycling in the cell and cleaning the cell of toxic materials that can accumulate. Other scientists took these studies even further and showed that diet and exercise also seem to trigger autophagy.

This research has profound implications for understanding cancer, too. It's a complicated issue, but autophagy is actually contributing to the disease and not helping the animal live longer. Still, if we can understand autophagy better through research, maybe we can understand how to cure cancer.

As a scientist, when I think about this possibility my eyes light up. When there is a medical breakthrough, as in treating cancer, we hear about it in the news. People get excited and want to know: What happens next? When can we begin applying this new knowledge or technique? They want to cure disease and save lives—as well they should. But these discoveries are often the result of many years of research by multiple teams of people. And it starts with basic research like ours.

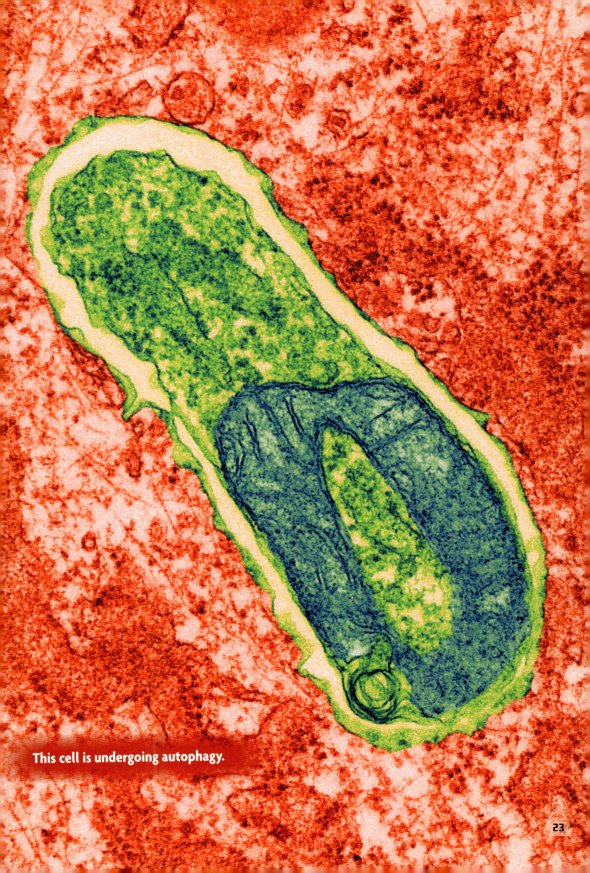

This cell is undergoing autophagy.

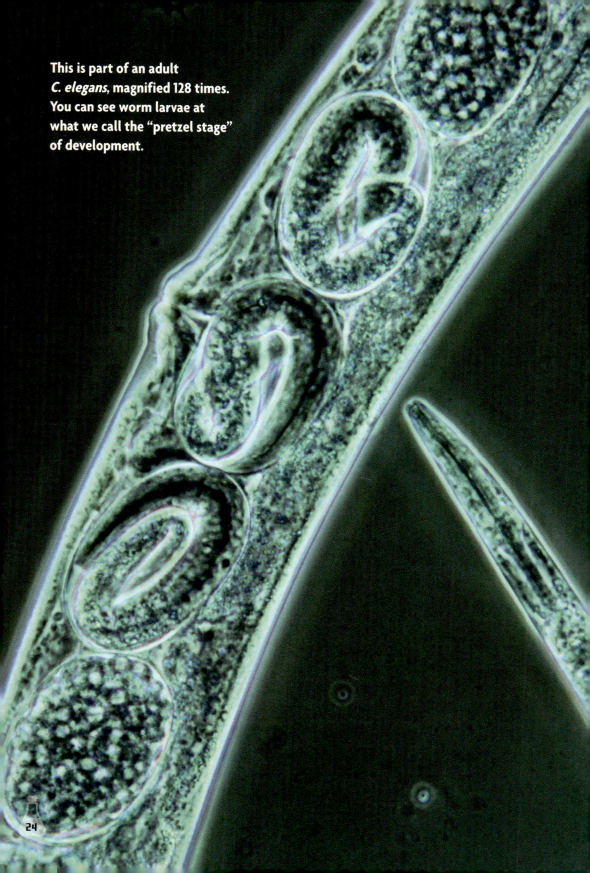

This is part of an adult *C. elegans*, magnified 128 times. You can see worm larvae at what we call the "pretzel stage" of development.

This is a different way of thinking because a lot of people believe that medical research on humans is the only kind that should be done. Yet if you tried these experiments with only humans it would take too long to get results. You simply couldn't do it. On the other hand, you *can* do this type of research with worms. It only takes three days for an egg to develop into an adult. So you can see why I truly believe that basic research is very important. What we discover in my little Lab D311/D315 at Queens College could have really profound implications for understanding how the human body works, too.

As you can tell, I love my work, so of course I am always thinking toward the future. I am always looking forward to new projects. I am always trying to establish new types of research using the worms.

I'm getting ready to begin an experiment.

My Family

I am proof that a woman can be a scientist and also raise a family. I have two sons, Paolo, age sixteen, and Lucas, who is nine. My eldest, he gets offended every time I say he's not passionate about science. He loves to study different languages, history, and political science. But who knows! Maybe he will also end up in the sciences like his mother and father. On the other hand, my little one is into natural science. He must have the science gene! He wants to know all about animals—where do they live, what do they eat?

Our family is very active. We go sailing and hiking together, and we like to go different places and have fun.

I almost forgot my *other* job: soccer mom. I go to lots of soccer games and soccer practices with my sons!

Here we are in Yosemite National Park. We hiked up to Glacier Point.

Here I am with my mother and brothers in New York. I am glad they get to visit on special occasions.

Succeeding in Science and Beyond

I was lucky growing up. I had the support of my family and many teachers, who gave me encouragement to pursue my interests. In some ways, life was simpler for me as a kid in San Juan than it is for some kids now—especially in New York City.

high school students at the American Museum of Natural History in New York City

But there are more opportunities now for young people interested in science. There are even opportunities for high school students to do lab research! When you do the research yourself, hands-on, step-by-step, it's just more fascinating than when you read about it in a book.

I am now a mentor, and a very proud one, too. This photo, taken at the 2013 Queens College graduation, shows me with my student Sara Wong. She worked in my lab beginning in her sophomore year, and graduated as the class valedictorian—the number one student! Sara went on for a graduate degree at the University of Michigan.

I also think it's important for any young person interested in science to find a mentor. You need people who have come before you in your field of study, who know the ropes of how to succeed. I was so fortunate to have that in college and even after. One of my mentors was a professor I met in college, Dr. Iva Greenwald. We developed such a strong relationship that I followed her to Columbia University to do my research.

Finding a mentor is extremely important for a young scientist.

Dr. Greenwald has probably been the most influential person in my scientific life. After all these years we are still friends, and we still communicate constantly! I send her my papers to review before they are published. I even send her my grant applications to read and help make better. It is so fantastic when there is someone willing to help you, or to give you a break in some way, such as mentioning your name when an opportunity arises. All these things, little by little, help a young person become successful.

Humility is another key to success, I think. Humility can be tough to maintain, because it seems that people who are better self-promoters get farther. But when you are humble, in my opinion, you are being honest, and striving to be better—and in the end, you will succeed.

Most of all, you must be persistent to withstand challenges and reach your goals. Maybe that is something that has also helped me as a woman of color. I often surprise people when I tell them I am a scientist; their reactions (both positive and negative) motivate me.

All these things have helped me as a scientist, but it's not really different for any other career. It helps to have something you are passionate about. But even then, as with anything else, the most important keys to success are to be strong and believe in yourself. And of course, to work hard.